MONONUCLEOSIS

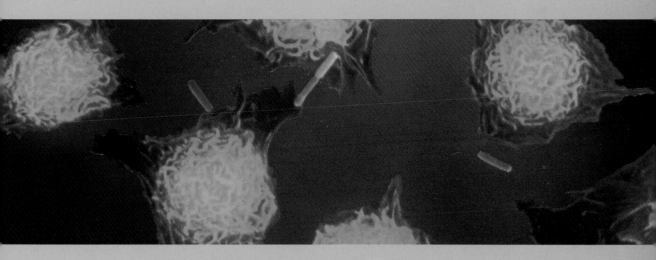

MONONUCLEOSIS

Gretchen Hoffmann

Marshall Cavendish
Benchmark
New York

Marshall Cavendish Benchmark
99 White Plains Road
Tarrytown, New York 10591-9001
www.marshallcavendish.us

This book is not intended for use as a substitute for advice, consultation, or treatment by a licensed medical practitioner. The reader is advised that no action of a medical nature should be taken without consultation with a licensed medical practitioner, including action that may seem to be indicated by the contents of this work, since individual circumstances vary and medical standards, knowledge, and practices change with time. The publisher, author, and medical consultants disclaim all liability and cannot be held responsible for any problems that may arise from use of this book.

Library of Congress Cataloging-in-Publication Data

Hoffmann, Gretchen.
  Mononucleosis / by Gretchen Hoffmann.
    p. cm. — (Health alert)
  Summary: "Discusses mononucleosis and its effects on people and society"—Provided by publisher.
  Includes index.
  ISBN 0-7614-1915-2
  1. Mononucleosis—Juvenile literature. I. Title. II. Series: Health alert
(Benchmark Books)

  RC147.G6.H645 2006
  616.9'1122—dc22   2005005001

Front cover: Epstein-Barr virus
Title page: Macrophages and bacteria

Photo research by Candlepants, Incorporated
Front cover: Prof. M.A. Epstein / Photo Researchers, Inc.
The photographs in this book are used by permission and through the courtesy of: *Photo Researchers Inc. Dr.* Gopal Murti, 3, 11, 22; Nibsc, 12; Steve G. Scheissner, 17; Institute Pasteur/Unite des Virus Oncongenes, 19; G. Tompkinson, 28; Science Photo Library, 36; Steve Allan, 37; Mauro Fermariello, 39; PHANIE, 40; Tek Image, 41; Maximilian Stock Ltd., 42; Scott Camazine, 43; Will & Demi McIntyre, 45; Doug Martin, 49; J. King Holmes, 55; Professor M.A. Epstein, 57. *Phototake:* John Karapelou, CMI, 15. *Getty Images:* PhotoDisc Green, 25; Time & Life Pictures, 31. *Corbis:* Jose Luis Pelaez, 27, Hulton-Deutsch, 35, Michael Keller, 50, Tom & Dee McCarthy, 53. *Greystone-Central News Photo/ Courtesy Alan Mason Chesney Medical Archives, Johns Hopkins Medical Institution:* 32. *The Image Works:* Bob Daemmrich, 47.

Printed in China

6 5 4 3 2

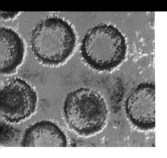

CONTENTS

WHAT IS IT LIKE TO HAVE MONONUCLEOSIS?

Like many people, Amy, a sixth grader, liked to sleep in on the weekends. But just a few weeks after her spring break, she started to feel like she could never get enough rest. Even twelve hours each night on the weekends was not enough to make the tiredness go away.

Amy was very busy, so she figured that she was just tired from schoolwork and her activities. But soon Amy was falling asleep on the couch when she got home from school. She even started sleeping through dinner and falling asleep while watching her favorite television shows. After a week of being very tired, Amy noticed that her throat and neck were very sore. A few days later, her neck was very swollen. It actually felt like she had softballs in her neck!

Amy went to her doctor to find out what was wrong. He felt her neck and realized that Amy's **glands** were swollen. The doctor also noticed that Amy had a fever. Some of Amy's blood was tested. Through these blood tests, her doctor confirmed that Amy had infectious mononucleosis.

Infectious mononucleosis—which is sometimes called mono—is a very common illness in young people. Although each person can have a different combination of symptoms—or signs of the illness—Amy experienced a few of the most common symptoms. These include a sore throat, swollen glands, and extreme tiredness. There is no cure for mono, but there are ways to treat the symptoms and make recovery more bearable.

The most important treatment is to rest and allow your body to fight the infection. Amy had to stay home from school until she regained her strength and the swelling in her glands went down. She got plenty of sleep, drank a lot of water and juice, and took pain relievers for her fever and sore throat.

About ten days after she saw her doctor, Amy started to feel more like her normal self again. But her doctor told her to continue to take it easy, because doing too much too soon can cause the symptoms to come back. Amy went back to school, but did not participate in after-school activities and sat out during gym class. Amy's doctor did not want her to become too tired with too much physical activity.

Amy continued to eat healthy foods and get plenty of sleep at night. About a month after finding out she had mono, she felt much better. Her doctor checked on her and told her she could go back to doing after-school and physical activities—but not too much. After a few more weeks, Amy was feeling great. She was able to do all the things she did before she had mononucleosis.

WHAT IS MONONUCLEOSIS?

Mononucleosis is an infectious disease caused by a **virus.** A virus is a microorganism that causes many diseases in humans, animals, and plants. Mono most commonly affects teenagers and young adults, and is best known for the way it takes away a person's energy. A person with mono can feel so tired that even everyday tasks, like brushing his or her hair or carrying a backpack full of books, can become exhausting. This extreme tiredness is called fatigue. Other symptoms of mono include having a fever, a sore throat, and swollen **lymph glands,** usually in the neck. A person with mono may also have headaches, a loss of appetite, skin rash, muscle aches, and an enlarged **spleen.** Sometimes it can take months to fully recover from a severe—serious—case of mono.

Mono is usually passed from person to person through direct contact with saliva—commonly referred to as spit.

Saliva is produced by the salivary glands, which are located on the insides of your cheeks and under your tongue. That is why sharing a cup, fork, spoon, straw, or food—anything that touches a sick person's mouth—can lead to catching mono. To fully understand how mono makes a person sick, it is important to know the basics about how the body defends itself against infection.

The Kissing Disease

....

Mono is sometimes called "the kissing disease," because kissing someone is an easy way to share saliva and become infected. But the kissing disease is a misleading nickname because kissing is definitely not the only way to pass saliva between people. Other actions that can transfer the virus from one person to another include

- Eating food from the same plate
- Sharing spoons or forks
- Drinking from the same cup
- Passing around and drinking from the same water bottle after sports practice
- Sipping from the same straw
- Brushing your teeth with someone else's toothbrush
- Using someone else's lip gloss
- Playing another person's musical instrument, like a clarinet or trumpet
- Small children putting another child's toy into their mouths

THE IMMUNE SYSTEM

The immune system is a body system that works to protect the body from **infection.** Anything unfamiliar to your body is considered a foreign substance. If this foreign substance triggers a response from your immune system it is called an **antigen.** Infection-causing **microbes** or germs, such as **bacteria,** viruses, or parasites can be antigens. The immune system is incredibly complex. It can recognize millions of different antigens. It takes several different types of cells, organs, and specialized chemicals working as a team to effectively protect the body from infection.

White Blood Cells

The most important cells working in the immune system are white blood cells, which are also called **leukocytes.** They circulate in the blood so that they can be quickly transported to an area where an infection has developed. There are several types of leukocytes that work to destroy intruding germs. The first type is a **phagocyte,** and its job is to find and destroy sources of infection. Phagocytes are large white blood cells that actually "eat" microbes by surrounding or engulfing them. The phagocytes then digest the microbes using enzymes, which are **proteins** that break the invader into small, harmless pieces. This process is called **phagocytosis.**

Phagocytes are able to identify their next "meal" through the help of another type of white blood cell called **lymphocytes.** There are two main types of lymphocytes: the B-cells and T-cells. B-cells produce **antibodies.** An antibody is a protein

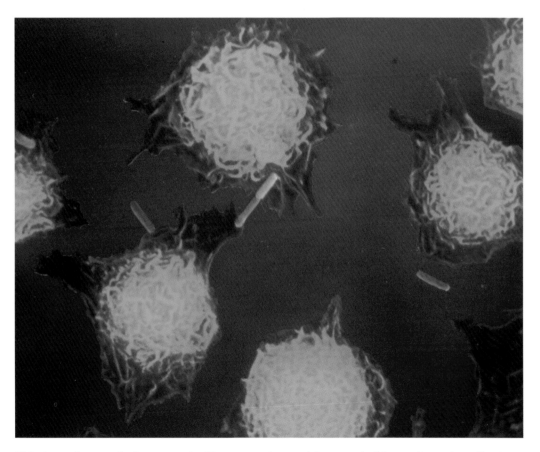

This is an image of phagocytosis. The macrophages (the round objects shown in yellow) are engulfing and killing foreign bacteria (shown as blue cylindrical objects) that have entered the body. The bacteria has the potential to cause illnesses and other health problems.

specially created by a B-cell to stick to a specific bacteria or virus. Antibodies do not actually kill the bacteria or virus. Instead, they mark whatever they are stuck to for destruction by phagocytes and other cells. B-cells are the main immune cells infected by the mononucleosis virus.

The other type of lymphocyte, the T-cells, coordinate the responses of other cells in the immune system. T-cells also participate in the direct attack. There are two main types of

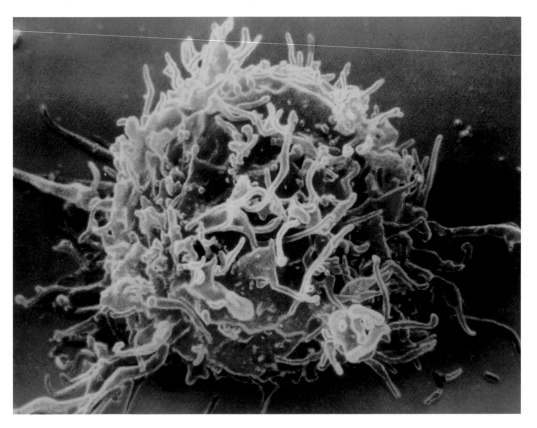

An enlarged look at a white blood cell. This is a normal T-cell, also called a T lymphocyte.

T-cells that have different but equally important jobs. Cells called helper T-cells direct and regulate the immune response by communicating with other immune cells. They help organize and motivate other cells to do their jobs. Another type of T-cell is called a killer T-cell or a cytotoxic T-cell. ("Cyto" means cell, and "toxic" means harmful, so "cytotoxic" means "cell-harming.") Cytotoxic cells directly attack the infected cells.

So how do T-cells know which B-cells are healthy, productive immune defenders and which ones are sick and infected? Infected B-cells display parts of the virus or bacteria (usually pieces of protein) on their surface. By doing that, it is almost like the B-cells are waving a big red flag that says, "SOMETHING IS WRONG WITH ME" to attract the attention of circulating helper T-cells. This signal tells the T-cell that the B-cell has something foreign and probably dangerous inside and needs to be destroyed. This puts helper T-cells into combat mode, and they release chemicals called **cytokines.** These chemical messengers tell nearby B-cells to start making more antibodies in a hurry. The antibodies will tell the phagocytes to start their feeding frenzy, killing the infected cells. The chemical messages also tell the cytotoxic T-cells to seek and destroy the infected B-cells.

Often, immune cells are good at remembering things. After some T-cells and B-cells are exposed to a specific bacteria or virus, they can remember that infection for a long time. These special memory cells are able to recognize a virus or bacteria that they have fought before. The next time the infection starts, the cells know to quickly attack and crush the infection. The body can respond much faster the second time it encounters the same virus because of the quick response of memory cells.

The Spleen, the Thymus, and Bone Marrow

In addition to white blood cells, the immune system includes several organs that defend the body from infection. A very important organ is the spleen. The spleen is located in the upper left side of the abdomen. (The abdomen is the area of your body below your chest, but above your hips.) The spleen's job is to filter blood. The spleen removes impurities from the blood or from other fluids in the body. Immune cells gather in the spleen and there they can meet and destroy these harmful substances.

Two organs with important roles in producing white blood cells are the thymus and bone marrow. The thymus is located in the center of the upper chest. It is the site where T-cells multiply and mature. The mature T-cells are transported from the thymus (through blood) to other parts of the body.

Bone marrow is the spongy filling inside your bones. The marrow produces all types of blood cells including B-cells. These blood cells are then carried away to other parts of the body through blood. Blood vessels run through the marrow,

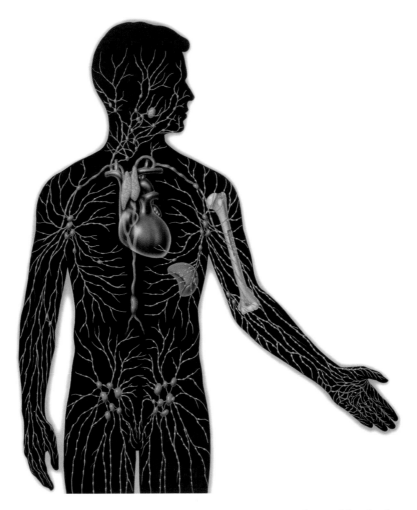

This illustration highlights some of the different parts of the body used by the immune system. The yellow structure above the heart (in the upper chest) is the thymus. The green vessels are lymph vessels that are linked to the green, bean-shaped stuctures called lymph nodes.

transporting blood cells and nutrients. There is an easy trick to remembering where the two different types of lymphocytes are made: **T**-cells come from the **t**hymus, and **B**-cells come from the **b**one marrow.

THE LYMPHATIC SYSTEM

An important part of the immune system is actually a separate body system. The lymphatic system plays a vital role in an immune response. This system shares many organs and cell types with the immune system, including the spleen and lymphocytes. The lymphatic system is made up of a network of organs, tissues, lymph nodes (also called lymph glands), and vessels that produce and transport a fluid called lymph throughout the body. Lymph fluid bathes all the cells in your body, and clears away dead cells and any other unusable substances that build up. The clear lymph is made up of proteins, fats, some red blood cells, and many white blood cells, especially lymphocytes. Lymphocytes continually pass back and forth between lymph tissue, lymph fluid, and blood.

Lymphatic fluid is carried in vessels, much like your blood is. At certain points in the body, the vessels connect to lymph nodes, which are like checkpoints that filter the fluid and remove foreign material, such as viruses. Lymph nodes are small, bean-shaped, and are located in clusters throughout the body. There are many lymph nodes located in the back of the head, sides of the neck, behind the ears, under the chin and jaw, and in the groin and armpits.

In fact, each person has between 500 and 1,500 lymph nodes. Immune cells also group together in lymph nodes—as they do in the spleen—because it is a good place to confront and destroy germs floating in the lymph.

This is a microscopic look inside a lymph node. White blood cells are shown in pink and red blood cells are shown in red. The yellowish-brown structures are macrophages.

Lymph nodes are usually soft and cannot easily be seen or felt. However, when the body is fighting an infection, lymph glands can become swollen and tender. The same is true for the tonsils. Tonsils are an example of lymphatic tissue in the throat. When you have certain infections, your tonsils can become enlarged. Sometimes tonsils can more than double or triple their normal size. If enlarged tonsils interfere with breathing, doctors might prescribe a special medication to help clear a person's airways. If a person's tonsils become too large, doctors sometimes consider removing them through surgery. But usually lymph nodes will go back to their normal size after an infection passes.

THE EPSTEIN-BARR VIRUS

The human body uses the combined defenses of the immune and lymphatic systems to destroy infectious invaders. In the case of mononucleosis, that invader is a virus. The organism the virus infects is called the host. The virus is considered a parasite and relies on the host to live and reproduce. There are many different types of viruses and they cause a variety of illnesses.

When a virus enters a person's body, it infects a cell and takes control of the cell. The virus tells the cell what to do and forces the cell to help replicate, or make copies of, the virus. These copies build up and eventually burst out of the cell. These new viruses circulate through the body to infect and destroy other cells.

Several types of viruses can cause mononucleosis-like symptoms. But approximately 90 percent of mononucleosis cases are caused by a single type of virus called the Epstein-Barr virus. The Epstein-Barr virus is a member of the

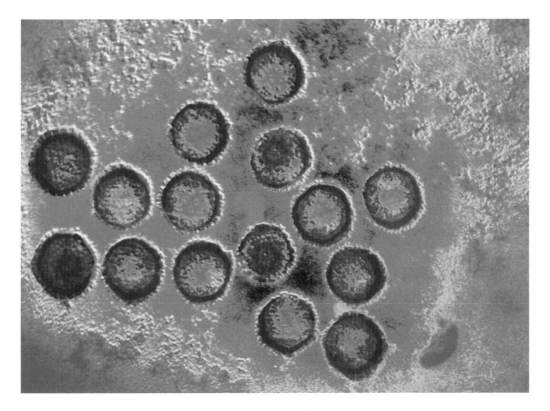

An electron micrograph of Epstein-Barr virus particles.

herpesvirus family. Its close relatives include the viruses that cause cold sores and chicken pox, and a virus known as cytomegalovirus. This virus can cause symptoms similar to Epstein-Barr mononucleosis.

The Epstein-Barr virus first infects the cells lining the mouth and throat. Next it moves onto the B-cells that have been sent to fight the infection. The infected B-cells are activated and produce a flood of antibodies. These antibodies are usually grouped into two types. One type specifically targets the Epstein-Barr virus. The other type includes more general antibodies called **heterophile antibodies.** Heterophile antibodies do not recognize the virus, and appear to be produced because of the disorder and chaos inside the infected B-cell. The presence of heterophile antibodies often helps medical professionals determine if a person has mononucleosis.

The Epstein-Barr virus infects up to 10 percent of the total B-cell population in the human body. It takes two to three weeks for the cytotoxic T-cells to find and destroy almost all of the B-cells infected with the Epstein-Barr virus. Usually, the T-cells are able to get the infection under control.

But this process is not perfect, and some infected B-cells are still left. The T-cells do not recognize these B-cells as infected cells, so it is almost like the infected B-cells are invisible to the immune system. These cells become **immortalized**, which means the virus stays inside them forever. When an immortalized B-cell divides into two new cells, each of those cells will also have the virus inside them. Through this process, the virus will continue to live inside the person for his or her entire life. However, this does not mean that the person will always have the symptoms of mono. The virus in immortalized cells stays dormant, or inactive, and the person is still considered healthy.

HOW COMMON IS INFECTION?

The Epstein-Barr virus cannot live for very long outside the host that it has infected, and is not found floating free in the environment. Even so, it is one of the most common viruses in the world. Experts believe that the Epstein-Barr virus will infect more than 90 percent of all people on Earth sometime during their lives. If the Epstein-Barr virus causes mononucleosis, and almost everyone gets infected with the virus, then everyone should get sick with mononucleosis at some point, right?

Wrong. Only a small percentage of people who become infected with the Epstein-Barr virus ever develop symptoms of mononucleosis. Some people can carry the virus in their

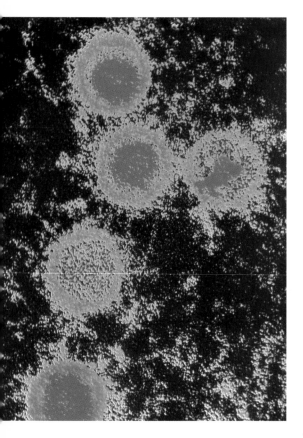

A very strong microscope shows the mononucleosis virus. The virus is too small to be seen with the naked eye.

bodies in the immortalized B-cells throughout their entire lives and never get sick. Why? It all depends on when that person developed immunity to the virus.

A person who is immune to the Epstein-Barr virus will not get sick if he or she encounters the virus again. For example, a person who has developed immunity to Epstein-Barr virus as a very young child will not develop mononucleosis as a teenager or as an adult when infected with the virus again. This is because young children exposed to the Epstein-Barr virus can usually fight off the infection without getting the classic symptoms of mononucleosis. They may only have minor symptoms that their parents and doctor disregard as a common cold or flu. They might not get sick at all. The virus will then stay in their bodies in an inactive form for the rest of their lives. But the antibodies against the virus will also stay in the body, helping to prevent these people from getting sick with mononucleosis.

Mono Around the World

It is oten the case that most infectious diseases, such as HIV (an immune system disease), tuberculosis (a respiratory disease), and cholera (an intestinal disease), are more frequently found in less-developed or developing countries. (An undeveloped nation is one that has much poverty and a lack of modern technological advances.) Mononucleosis is an infectious disease and can affect a person just about anywhere in the world. But unlike many other infectious diseases, mono is actually much more common in developed nations. Less developed countries tend to have fewer cases of mononucleosis.

Why is this so? Less developed countries often have poor systems for providing clean water and disposing of waste properly. This makes people more likely to become infected by bacteria and viruses. (Diseases such as tuberculosis and cholera are most often spread in such environments.) This also exposes people to a larger number of viruses, such as the Epstein-Barr virus. But unlike other infectious diseases, getting exposed to the Epstein-Barr virus early in life may actually be beneficial. Because children in developing countries are usually exposed to Epstein-Barr by the age of four or five, they develop early immunity and never get mononucleosis in their teens.

The same idea is true in modernized countries like the United States, which still have a percentage of people who live in close quarters or in unsanitary conditions. These people are much more likely to be exposed to the virus at a very young age, will develop immunity, and will never experience mononucleosis later in life.

This may explain why certain nations have more cases of mononucleosis, but it does not mean that living in unclean conditions or being exposed to infectious bacteria or viruses are good things. Practicing good hygiene (maintaining cleanliness and good health) and living in a clean environment are important to being healthy. However, many people in the world do not have a choice about where they live or the environmental conditions that affect them. Unfortunately, this usually means that they are more likely to be affected by dangerous or deadly diseases.

However, if someone contracts the virus for the first time as a teenager, and he or she does not already have antibodies able to recognize and fight the virus, the person is more likely to get sick. This is because the risk of Epstein-Barr infection developing into mononucleosis increases with age. For example, the percentage of teenagers who develop mononucleosis is as much as 100 times higher than the percentage of children younger than five who develop the illness.

Although mononucleosis most commonly affects young people between the ages of 15 and 24, it can be found in much younger children and in adults in their thirties. In fact, approximately 1 in 500 adolescents and young adults in the United States will develop mononucleosis each year, and it might be as many as 1 in 200.

You might think that it is easy to avoid getting mononucleosis by simply not coming into contact with a sick person. While it is good to avoid people who have the symptoms, it is not that simple. The tricky part about the Epstein-Barr virus is that a person does not need to have the symptoms in order to spread the virus. From time to time, some of the virus leaves the immortalized B-cells and can spread to other people through saliva. This is why it is almost impossible to prevent the spread of the virus. Healthy people who are already immune to the disease are the most common cause of new cases of mononucleosis (in new people).

Another factor that makes it difficult to avoid infection is the viral incubation period. This is the period where the virus is replicating and spreading inside the body. During this time, the newly-infected person does not show any signs of being sick. The Epstein-Barr virus has a long incubation period of 30 to 50 days. This means that during this time, an infected person— who does not know that he or she is about to develop mononucleosis—can give the virus to someone else without knowing it.

SYMPTOMS

Even when a person infected with the Epstein-Barr virus does develop mononucleosis, he or she does not always experience the same set of symptoms as other people who have had mono. Individuals may experience

A fever is a common symptom of viral infections. Doctors describe a fever as a rise in normal body temperature.

all or only some of the symptoms associated with the disease.

Fatigue, malaise (a non-specific "sick" feeling), and weakness are similar terms to describe the same symptom of infectious mononucleosis—feeling completely drained of energy. Usually patients with mono feel most tired during the first two or three weeks of the illness. Some people feel so tired that they cannot get out of bed all day. Or, they might not be able to complete their normal activities, like taking a shower or walking the dog, without feeling exhausted. Like all mononucleosis symptoms, how bad the fatigue is and how long it lasts, is different for every person.

During the initial one to two weeks of illness, most people have a fever. Body temperatures usually peak in the early afternoon or early evening at approximately 103 degrees Fahrenheit. Some fevers may reach as high as 105 degrees. An average temperature for a healthy person is usually around 98.6 degrees.

Pharyngitis, or sore throat, is also a common symptom of mononucleosis. It is usually worse during the first five to seven days, but typically improves after ten days. It may be quite severe, and can make swallowing, talking, and eating painful. There may also be a whitish coating on the throat and tonsils.

Swollen glands are another part of having mononucleosis. Lymph glands are often swollen when a person has mono. Tonsils or lymph glands in the neck can be swollen, causing a sore neck. In most cases, swollen lymph glands will return to their normal size after the third or fourth week of infection.

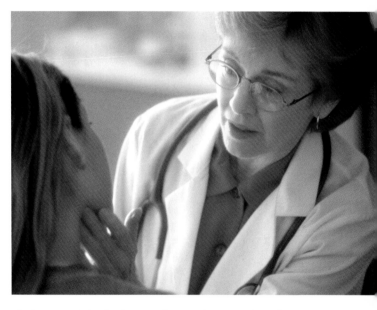

A doctor might feel around your throat and neck area to see if your glands are swollen. Swollen glands are a sign that your body is fighting an infection.

Other organs can also become swollen during mononucleosis, and the most common is the spleen. Researchers estimate that between 50 to 100 percent of mono patients develop an enlarged spleen. Why? When a person has mononucleosis the spleen works overtime, filtering viral particles and dead cells out of the blood. This extra demand for a strong immune response causes the spleen to become swollen and tender. The official term for this condition is **splenomegaly**. The spleen usually returns to normal size about a month after infection.

How does a doctor know if a patient's spleen is enlarged? In some cases, the spleen becomes so swollen that the doctor can simply feel it sticking out just by pressing on parts of the abdomen. Other more sophisticated tests, such as an ultrasound, can help doctors more accurately determine the size of the spleen. An ultrasound uses high-frequency sound waves to painlessly create images of organs and systems within the body. In this case, sound waves are aimed into the abdomen from a handheld device. The waves

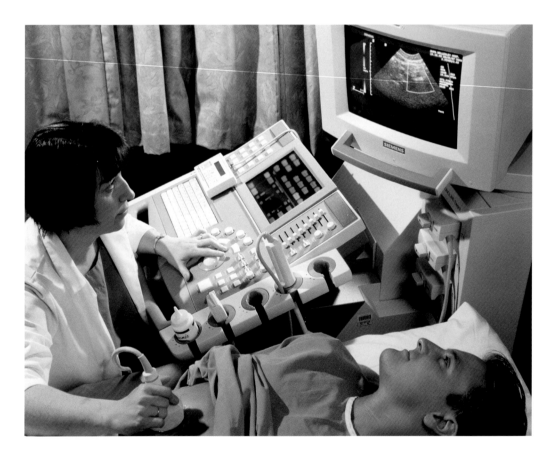

A doctor uses an ultrasound machine to view a patient's abdomen. Ultrasounds are ideal for looking at organs and other structures inside the body.

bounce off the organs and are received by a computer that uses them to create a picture of the shape and position of the organs.

The seriousness and type of mono symptoms can be different depending on what age group the patient is in. Swollen lymph nodes and sore throat are more common symptoms in patients younger than 35 years old. A patient older than 40 is more likely to have a longer-lasting fever and an enlarged liver as the most common symptoms. But many patients and doctors might assume that these symptoms are from the flu or some other common illness, instead of mono. This is just one more reason why mononucleosis can sometimes be more difficult to recognize in adult patients.

3

THE HISTORY OF MONONUCLEOSIS

Mononucleosis has probably affected the human race for thousands of years. But until scientists and doctors learned more about the human body and how its systems worked, mononucleosis could not be identified or treated effectively.

During the 1880s, German doctors first described a syndrome characterized by general malaise, fever, sore throat, and enlarged lymph nodes. The sickness occurred mostly in children, and usually only lasted a short time. This condition became known as glandular fever. Medical literature continued to refer to this rather vague illness until 1920, when doctors renamed it based on a physical characteristic of the illness.

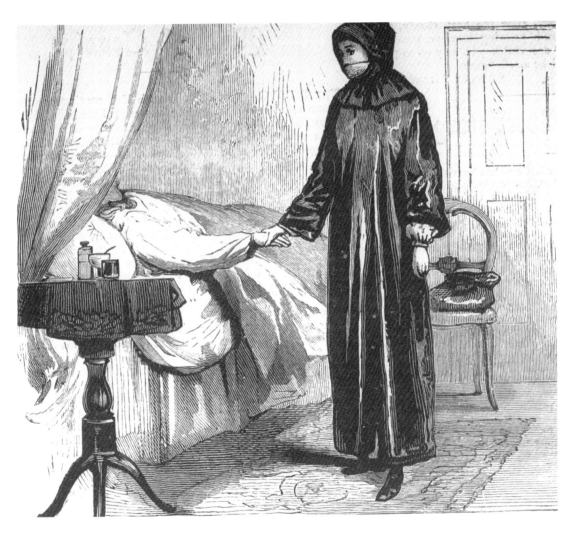

A fever is a symptom of many different diseases, and humans have been dealing with fevers for thousands of years. As scientists learned more about the human body and the cells within, they found ways to treat the fevers—and the illnesses causing them.

Dr. Thomas Sprunt

NAMING AND IDENTIFYING THE DISEASE

Those doctors were Thomas Sprunt and Frank Evans from Johns Hopkins University in Maryland. Dr. Sprunt and Dr. Evans took blood samples from students with fever, swollen lymph nodes, and fatigue—the same types of symptoms as glandular fever. When they examined the blood under a microscope, they saw an unusually large number of white blood cells called mononuclear lymphocytes. They renamed the illness *infectious mononucleosis* because of the large number of these cells.

In 1932, a better way to diagnose mononucleosis was discovered by Dr. John Paul and Dr. Walls Bunnell. They found that blood from human mononucleosis patients reacts unusually when it is mixed with blood from another animal, such as a sheep or a horse. But why would these scientists think that mixing blood from sick patients with the blood from sheep would be an interesting experiment to try? Their reason was that other doctors had figured out that antibodies from one species of animal could be used to test for diseases in other species. They were using this technique to try to find out more about mononucleosis. What they found was that combining a sick patient's blood and sheep blood caused big clumps to form.

The clumps are made of red blood cells sticking together. These clumps are large enough to be seen through a micro-scope. The red blood cells are stuck together because of heterophile antibodies floating in the mononucleosis patient's blood. Human heterophile antibodies are attracted to blood cells from a different animal—in this case red blood cells from the sheep. The heterophile antibodies attack the foreign sheep cells causing a reaction that makes the cells stick together in a clumpy mass.

This reaction is the basis of one of the most important tests for diagnosing mononucleosis: the heterophile antibody test, or the Monospot test. Newer versions of this test are still used today and they show the reac-tion between the human antibodies and red blood cells from a different animal. Doctors deter-mine whether or not a person has mononucleo-sis based on the

Before Dr. Sprunt and Dr. Evans renamed mononucleosis, some doctors confused the illness with a much more serious cancer of the white blood cells called **leukemia.** Although in both leukemia and mononucleosis there are an abnormally high number of white blood cells, the cells in mononucleosis have bizarre and unique shapes that are all different, while leukemia cells all look pretty much the same. Doctors rarely mistake mononucleosis for leukemia today.

presence of the clumps. A positive result (formation of clumps) tells doctors that the body is actively fighting, or has recently fought, the virus.

FINDING A CAUSE

By the 1940s and 1950s, doctors knew what mononucleosis was and how to test for it, but they still did not know what caused infectious mononucleosis. Most doctors guessed it was a virus, but no one knew for sure.

The researchers who eventually solved the mystery were actually working on a different medical puzzle at the time. The story of how doctors discovered that the Epstein-Barr virus causes mononucleosis actually began with research done in Africa. In the late 1950s, a British doctor named Denis Burkitt was studying a specific type of tumor—clumps of fast-growing cells that can sometimes be dangerous—that was common in African children. Dr. Burkitt was very interested in these tumors, which could sometimes grow as large as baseballs in the children's jaws and necks. This illness was eventually named Burkitt's lymphoma in honor of Dr. Burkitt's work. Lymphomas are cancers of the lymphatic system. This particular lymphoma caught the interest of two researchers from London, who asked for samples of the tumor cells to study at their lab in London.

In 1964, scientists Michael Anthony Epstein and Yvonne Barr

used a very powerful microscope, called an electron microscope, to examine lymphoma
cells. They discovered what
they thought was a new virus.
They were the first to describe
this new member of the herpesvirus family, but they needed help to confirm that it was
actually a new virus. They sent
a sample of their discovery,
named the Epstein-Barr virus,
to viral researchers Werner and
Gertrude Henle in Philadelphia.

The Henles confirmed that
the Epstein-Barr virus was
indeed a virus that no one had
ever seen before. Next, they
got to work proving that this
new virus was associated with
Burkitt's lymphoma. They

A scientist uses an electron microscope in the 1950s.
The electron microscopes provided scientists with a
powerful tool that could be used in many different
fields of research.

found that the Epstein-Barr virus was present in all patients
with the lymphatic cancer. But surprisingly, it was also found in
healthy people who did not have cancer. In fact, when they

Dr. Michael Anthony Epstein

tested the blood of workers in their own lab, they found that nearly everyone tested positive for the antibodies.

The Henles believed that the virus was somehow connected to lymphatic cancer, but it also caused a different non-cancerous illness (which we now now is mononucleosis.)

Like many of the great discoveries of science, the answer was discovered by chance. A 19-year-old laboratory technician working in the Henle lab was the only one who had not tested positive for Epstein-Barr antibodies. In 1968, this young woman became ill with swollen glands, fever, sore throat, and fatigue. When she did not start to feel better after several weeks, she had a blood test to find out what was wrong. This time she tested positive for Epstein-Barr antibodies. In addition, the Henles saw many of the mononuclear lymphocytes described by Dr. Sprunt and Dr. Evans in the young woman's blood. She had mononucleosis, and the Henles figured out that Epstein-Barr virus had been the cause. The technician's unfortunate illness was the final piece in the mononucleosis puzzle, and helped solve this very old medical mystery.

MONONUCLEOSIS TODAY

Since the 1960s, medical centers around the world have continued to do research on infectious diseases like mononucleosis. Advanced technology and new information about how viruses behave has been extremely helpful. Stronger microscopes have allowed researchers to look more closely at viruses and the cells they affect.

Many laboratories and institutions are dedicated solely to the study of viruses. Researchers there are constantly learning new things and finding new ways to help prevent infectious diseases and treat people who are affected by them.

A scientist uses an electron microscope to view blood cells. Electron microscopes are still very large, but today's versions are far more powerful than earlier versions used in the past.

4

DIAGNOSING AND TREATING MONONUCLEOSIS

After researchers knew the Epstein-Barr virus causes mono, they were able to design tests that could determine if a patient really has mono or a similar illness. Diagnosing mono can help doctors treat their patients and possibly avoid health complications.

DIAGNOSIS

Having a fever, swollen glands, a sore throat, and feeling tired are typical symptoms of other illnesses. Mononucleosis is often mistaken for illnesses like the flu. To know for sure if a patient is suffering from mono, there are several tests that can be done in a laboratory. The first is called the Monospot test. Although it has been improved upon and made easier to administer since its initial discovery in the 1930s, it is still

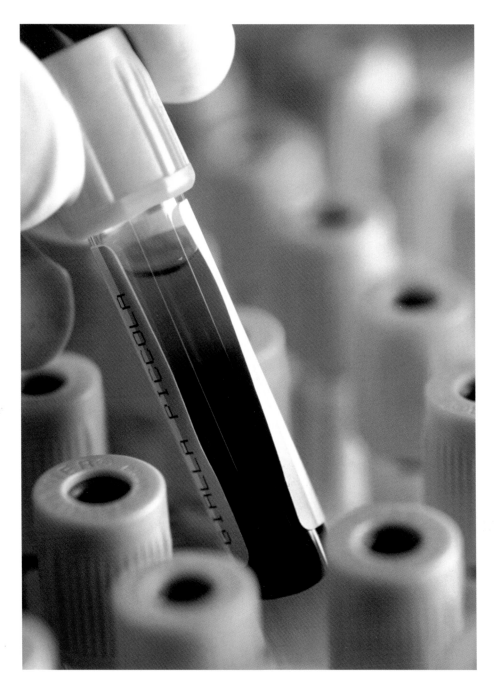

A laboratory technician selects a sample of blood stored in a special tube. Laboratories can test human blood for a variety of illnesses, including mononucleosis.

based on the original concept of testing a patient's blood with blood from nonhuman species, usually a sheep or a horse.

The test is a quick and mostly painless procedure. As in most blood tests, the nurse or doctor first cleans a small area on the back of the hand or inside of elbow to make sure the area is free of dirt and germs. Next, a small needle is used to collect blood from a vein in that area, and the blood is collected in a tube. The blood is then tested. The Monospot test is positive in approximately 85 to 90 percent of mononucleosis cases.

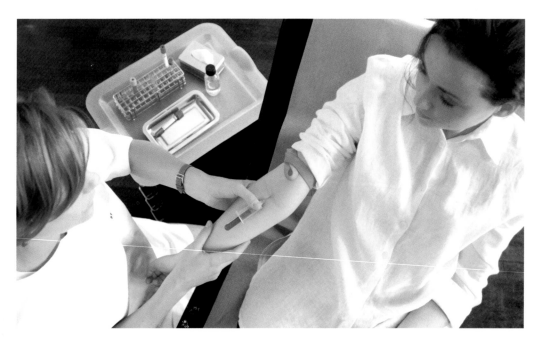

A nurse takes a sample of blood from a young patient. When done properly, blood drawing is relatively painless and simple.

A second type of diagnostic test is also a blood test called a complete blood count (CBC). In this test, the patient's blood is examined under a microscope to count the number of white blood cells. CBC tests are done to diagnose a number of different diseases or illnesses. In cases where mononucleosis is suspected, the doctor or laboratory technician looks for a certain type of white blood cell called mononuclear lymphocytes. Patients with mononucleosis have an increased number of mononuclear lymphocytes.

However, if neither the Monospot nor the CBC blood tests can confirm an Epstein-Barr infection, a test for

Monospot Testing

Though the Monospot test is usually accurate, sometimes the test results can be confusing. For example, a person who definitely has mono may have a first Monospot test result that is negative—which means that the result says that he or she is not infected. This is called a false-negative result. Sometimes the first test will be negative because the test was done too early in the illness for the antibodies to appear. If the patient is retested a week later, usually the second test will be positive because the antibodies have had time to build up and can be detected.

In other cases, the test will have a false-positive result. This means the patient will test positive for the antibodies, but not have an active case of mono. A false-positive result may occur because the antibodies can remain in the blood for up to nine months after a person is first infected.

A researchers looks at many samples of blood.

A laboratory technician uses a special machine called a Coulter counter. This machine analyzes blood and counts red and white blood cells.

virus-specific antibodies is the next step. This means that the laboratory will test the blood for specific antibodies that fight the Epstein-Barr virus. These virus-specific antibody tests are much more sophisticated, more expensive, and rarely necessary because such a high percentage of cases are diagnosed with the Monospot test.

COMPLICATIONS

Approximately 95 percent of mononucleosis patients feel much better in a few weeks. However, a small percentage of patients develop complications, which can be mild or very serious.

A relatively harmless complication is the development of another infection such as **streptococcal pharyngitis,** a bacterial throat infection commonly called strep throat, sinus infection, or tonsillitis. These are bacterial infections that can be treated with medication called antibiotics. However, taking certain medication to treat these infections may cause a pink skin irritation in someone who has mononucleosis. In fact, up to 90 percent of people with mononucleosis have this reaction to antibiotics. In cases where mononucleosis was not already suspected, this rash usually showed the doctor that the patient actually has mono and not just a bacterial infection.

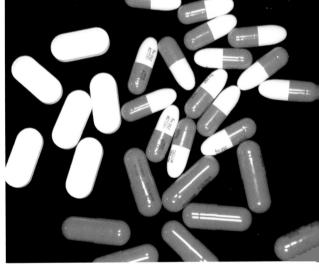

Antiobiotics are often prescribed to treat bacterial infections and other illnesses. Viral infections, however, cannot be treated with antibiotics.

One serious complication of mononucleosis is a ruptured, or burst, spleen. An enlarged spleen is more likely to burst if pressure is applied. This force can come from activity such as contact sports or simply lifting a heavy object, but it can also happen with very little activity. A spleen rupture usually feels like a sharp, sudden pain in the left, upper abdomen and may cause serious bleeding inside the abdomen. A ruptured spleen is considered a medical emergency and requires immediate medical attention. Doctors usually use surgery to remove a ruptured spleen.

While these and other complications are possible, it is important to remember that they only occur in less than 1 percent of people with mononucleosis. Death from mono occurs in less than 1 percent of patients and is usually due to a serious complication. It is rarely due to the actual mono infection.

Some rare complications of mononucleosis include several types of blood disorders or problems. Although the spleen is the most commonly affected organ, mononucleosis can cause problems in other organs such as the heart, the brain, and the liver. Nerves are bundles of fibers that receive and send messages between the body and the brain. Sometimes mono infections can result in nerve damage. This nerve damage may cause conditions such as seizures, which are disruptions of normal brain function that may cause abnormal body movements or behaviors. It may also cause Guillain-Barré syndrome, which involves temporary paralysis of some or all muscles. (Muscles are paralyzed when they cannot function or move.) However, Guillain-Barre syndrome usually reverses itself but leaves people weakened for a long time.

TREATMENT

Even without serious complications mononucleosis can be a prolonged condition that keeps you at home for weeks as you recover. The acute phase of the illness (when you have a sore throat, fever, swollen lymph glands and other symptoms) usually lasts about two

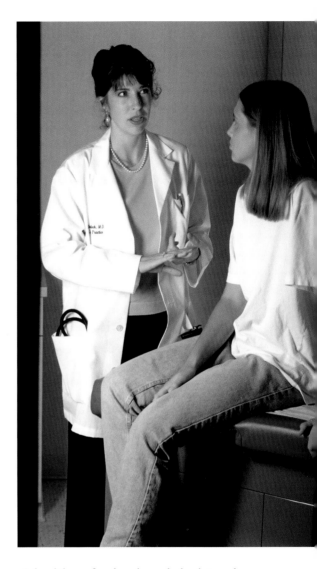

A health professional can help determine what you need to do when you are not feeling well. All young people—and even adults—should have regular check-ups to maintain a healthful life.

weeks. This is the period when a person with mono is most contagious, or most likely to spread the virus to other people. Approximately 20 percent of patients can return to work or school within one week of being diagnosed and about 50 percent can return within two weeks. But mononucleosis can also leave a person feeling very tired for a long time after the other symptoms have subsided. It may be two to three months before a person finally feels completely normal.

Isolating patients—keeping them somewhere away from other people—with mononucleosis is not necessary because spreading it requires direct exchange of infected saliva. You can live in the same house or be in the same classroom as people with the illness and never become infected with the virus. But you should still be careful not to come into contact with their saliva.

With all of the research that has been done on mononucleosis, and the specific tests designed to diagnose the illness, you might assume that doctors have found successful ways to treat, cure, or prevent this infectious disease. However, the treatments for mononucleosis have remained pretty much the same ever since the 1960s when doctors discovered that it was caused by the Epstein-Barr virus. Doctors still advise getting plenty of rest, drinking fluids, taking a non-aspirin pain reliever, and eating a well-balanced diet to treat the symptoms of the illness.

Antibiotics are not effective against viral infections, and antiviral drugs have not really worked in treating mononucleosis. Most treatment options are largely supportive, which means that the treatments simply deal with the symptoms. The treatments attempt to make the patient more comfortable. The virus is usually just left to run its course. This means

Resting and drinking enough fluids are important parts of recovering from many types of illness.

that in most cases doctors simply wait to see if a patient's immune system will be able to fight and beat the viral infection.

PHYSICAL ACTIVITY

Having mononucleosis means having to miss some activities, such as classes, team practices, and parties, because getting plenty of rest is the key to recovery. Many patients feel too weak to go to school or even walk around their house, and just feel like staying in bed. Bed rest is especially important for people with high fevers and muscle pains. The goal should be to allow the body to rest and recover. However, excessive bed rest can actually make symptoms of tiredness and weakness worse. This is because your body can become out of shape while just lying down in bed for long periods of time.

But people who are sick should not engage in too much physical activity. Not only can a person cause more injuries, but he or she might even make the illness worse. Patients need to find the right balance of rest and physical activity. A person who is sick needs to get enough rest, but he or she should also take part in enough physical activity to stay healthy. A medical professional can help a patient understand what the right balance should be.

A patient with an enlarged spleen has to be especially careful about heavy or rough physical activities. An enlarged spleen has a great chance or rupturing, so sports should be avoided for at least a month after the illness starts. If the spleen is very enlarged, a doctor might even recommend waiting as long as two months, just to be safe. However, a person with mono should always ask a doctor about restrictions on physical activity—whether or not the spleen is enlarged.

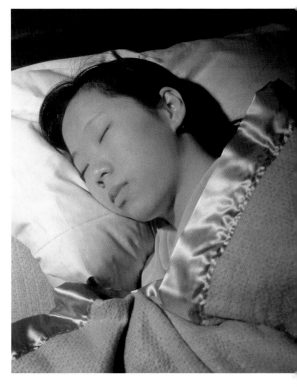

Getting the right amount of sleep can help a person fight off some illnesses and infections. Letting the body rest is necessary to keep the immune system strong.

Returning to your usual schedule too soon can increase the chance that you will become sicker. You need to be patient with your body as it fights the infection, and be aware of signs that you are doing too much. Patients often get bored or sad when they have mononucleosis, because they cannot enjoy their normal activities, such as sports, clubs, or other hobbies that they might be too tired to do. Try keeping occupied with relaxing activities, such as reading, watching movies, or listening to new types of music. Sketching or keeping a journal are also good options for passing the time. It is important to try to maintain a positive outlook, while still taking it slow to allow the body time to heal.

Foods such as fresh vegetables are necessary for a balanced and healthful diet.

DIET

Even though you might not feel hungry, you should try to eat healthful foods while battling mononucleosis. Fruits, vegetables, whole grains, and other similar foods will give your body essential vitamins and the energy it needs to continue fighting the virus. Medical professionals can help you figure out what kind of diet will be the most healthful.

It is important to drink plenty of fluids such as water and juice. This will prevent dehydration—the loss of too much water from the body. Drinking enough fluids can also help relieve fever and soothe a sore throat. Cool liquids, and even smoothies and popsicles, can help you get the fluids your body needs while soothing your throat at the same time.

PAIN MANAGEMENT

For sore throats, doctors often recommend gargling with warm salty water. You should ask a doctor or medical professional how much salt to use and how to gargle properly. Gargling several times each day can help make a sore throat feel better by cleaning out mucus and soothing inflamed areas. Sucking on throat lozenges (cough drops) or hard candy can also help provide some relief. But be very careful when sucking on lozenges or candy. Do not suck on lozenges while lying down or moving around or talking a lot—you might choke.

For muscle pains and headaches, your doctor might suggest taking an over-the-counter pain reliever. Over-the-counter medication does not require a doctor's prescription. These drugs can be bought easily at a pharmacy or grocery store. (Prescription medication requires a special note or

Reye's Syndrome

....

Description: Reye's syndrome is primarily a children's disease but can occur at any age. It is most harmful to the brain and the liver. It generally occurs in combination with a previous viral infection, such as the flu, chicken pox, or mononucleosis.

Symptoms: Vomiting, personality changes such as irritability or combativeness (arguing a lot), disorientation (confusion), convulsions, and loss of consciousness.

Cause: Unknown. However, studies have shown that using aspirin to treat viral illnesses increases the risk of developing Reye's syndrome.

Treatment: There is no cure, but when Reye's syndrome is diagnosed and treated in its early stages, chances of recovery are excellent.

order from a doctor.) Examples of over-the-counter pain relievers are ibuprofen or acetaminophen. Aspirin is another pain reliever, but doctors warn not to use it for this illness. This is because of the small risk of Reye's syndrome, a complication that results in organ failure and swelling of the brain. Reye's syndrome is not just associated with mononucleosis—it is also linked other viral infections such as chicken pox and influenza. Doctors make the same recommendation to avoid aspirin when treating these other illnesses. In general, you should never take a medication— prescription or over-the-counter— without consulting a doctor or medical professional.

STAYING HEALTHY

The Epstein-Barr virus is virtually impossible to avoid because it is spread by healthy people and more than 95 percent of the world's population is eventually infected. However, there are a few ways to reduce your chances of getting mononucleosis. The first is to have a healthy immune system. That means taking good care of your body. Exercise and getting enough sleep are essential to staying healthy. Eating well is also important. Taking multivitamins can help make sure your body is getting the vitamins and minerals it needs. A medical professional can help you determine which multivitamin is right for you.

Stress is also a big factor in weakening the immune system— unfortunately, it is often an unavoidable part of life. Trying

Schoolwork and other activities can be very stressful. It is important to find ways to reduce and manage your stress. Managing stress levels is one way to stay healthy.

to balance schoolwork, a job, friends, sports, and responsibilities at home can be very stressful and challenging and can wear a person down. This is especially true for high school and college students. Stress levels can be managed by making sure you do not participate in too much. A schedule that is too busy and filled with too much to do can make a person feel very stressed. Taking time for relaxing activities such as meditation or taking walks can help reduce stress levels. People who feel stressed may find comfort in talking about problems and concerns with family member, friends, or medical professionals. At school, students can talk to teachers and guidance counselors about stress.

THE FUTURE OF MONONUCLEOSIS

Scientists are working on new ways to prevent people from getting mononucleosis. They are trying to find an Epstein-Barr **vaccine.** A vaccine is a medical treatment that can help prevent certain illnesses. Vaccines can be made of part of a virus, a weakened version of it, or a manmade or altered version. People are given vaccines—usually through injections—so that their immune systems will know how to fight the illness. Immune cells recognize the vaccine as a foreign substance, and create antibodies to fight it. Some cells will

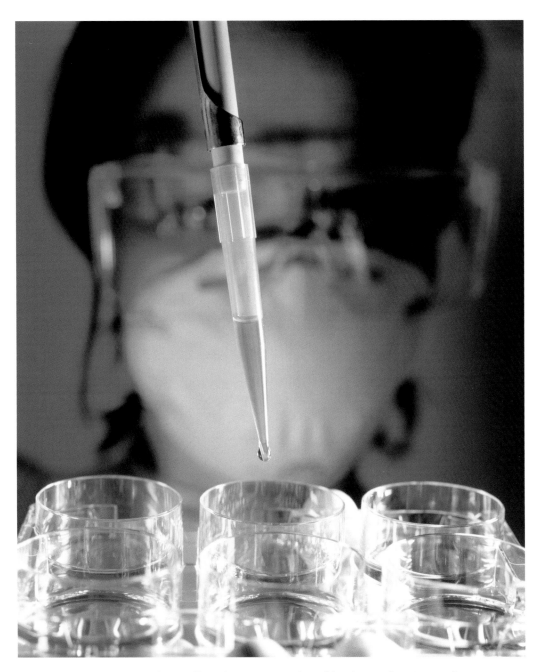

A virologist—a person who studies viruses—examines blood samples. Research centers that specialize in virology (the study of viruses) are working to understand how viruses affect us and what can be done to keep people safe and healthy.

always remember having seen the virus, and will be prepared to fight it again when there is a real infection. Vaccinations do not usually cause illness, though some people may experience slight symptoms.

Scientists have developed vaccines that help prevent illnesses such as chicken pox, polio, and the flu. If scientists are able to develop a successful Epstein-Barr vaccine, people might be protected from ever getting sick with mononucleosis.

But doctors are still working on a way to make a vaccine that is both safe and effective. They are learning more about why the virus specifically chooses to infect B lymphocytes. Researchers also need to be able to test the vaccine in animals to make sure that it is safe and effective before they can test it in humans. Usually other animals, such as mice, rats, and rabbits, are used for laboratory research, but up to now only monkeys have shown the ability to be infected with the Epstein-Barr virus. Further research is ongoing to create an effective system for testing possible vaccines.

Perhaps some day researchers will find a sure way to prevent mononucleosis infections. It is possible that they might even one day find a cure for it.

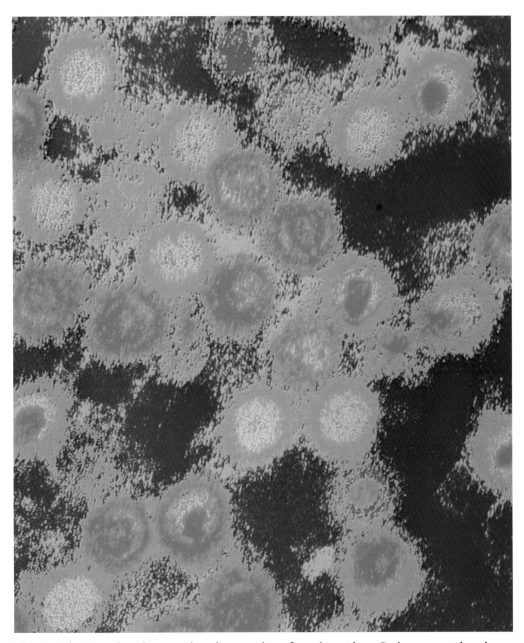

The Epstein-Barr virus has perplexed researchers for a long time. Perhaps sometime in the future, scientists will find a way to treat and control it.

GLOSSARY

antibody—A protein molecule produced by a B-cell in response to a foreign substance. It locks onto the substance and helps the body destroy or inactivate it.

antigen—A substance or molecule recognized by the immune system as potentially harmful.

bacteria—Microscopic organisms composed of a single cell. Some are actually beneficial and live inside the body, others can cause illness.

bone marrow—Soft tissue located inside bones. It is the source of all blood cells.

cytokines—Chemical substances that act as messengers to other cells.

enzyme—A protein produced by living cells that promotes a chemical process or reaction.

Epstein-Barr virus—A member of the herpesvirus family that causes mononucleosis.

glands—Parts inside the body that change substances found in blood into chemicals the body uses to function.

Guillain-Barré syndrome—A rare complication of mononucleosis involving weakness and temporary paralysis.

herpesvirus—One of a family of viruses including those that cause health problems that include chicken pox, cold sores, and mononucleosis.

heterophile antibodies—Antibodies produced against the cells of another species (such as a sheep).

immortalized—Will last forever—in the case of B-cells, it means the virus will last forever inside the cell and its descendants.

immunity—The ability to resist a disease.

infection—An illness caused by bacteria, viruses, parasites, or other harmful substances that enter the body.

leukemia—An uncontrolled growth in the number of white blood cells.

leukocytes—All white blood cells.

lymph glands—Also called lymph nodes, these are small, bean-shaped organs of the immune system located throughout the body and connected by lymphatic vessels. these are where disease-fighting white blood cells gather and where lymph fluid is filtered.

lymphadenopathy—An abnormal enlargement of the lymph nodes.

lymphocytes—Small white blood cells of two types: B- and T-cells.

microbes—Microscopic living organisms, such as bacteria and viruses.

myocarditis—Inflammation of the heart muscle.

parasites—Plants or animals that live, grow, and feed on or within another living organism without giving any benefit back.

phagocyte—Large white blood cell that can destroy microbes, other cells, and foreign particles by engulfing them.

phagocytosis—The process by which one cell engulfs a large particle or another cell.

protein—Substances found in living cells of plants and animals. Proteins are needed for cells to do their jobs.

spleen—A large abdominal organ that acts as a filter and holding tank for blood and immune cells.

splenomegaly—Enlargement of the spleen.

streptococcal pharyngitis—A bacterial infection of the throat—often called "strep throat."

thymus—A primary organ of the lymphatic system located in the chest. This is where T-cells grow and mature.

tonsils—Masses of lymph tissue in the throat. They can become enlarged when white blood cells are actively fighting an infection.

vaccine—A substance that is used to prevent illness or disease.

virus—A microorganism that causes many diseases and illness in humans, animals, and plants.

FIND OUT MORE

Books

Derkins, Susie. *The Immune System*. New York: The Rosen
  Publishing Group, 2001.

Gedatus, Gustav Mark. *Mononucleosis*. Mankato, MN:
  LifeMatters, 2000.

Silverstein, Alvin, Virginia Silverstein, and Robert
  Silverstein. *Mononucleosis*. Berkeley Heights, NJ: Enslow
  Publishers, Inc., 1994.

Smart, Paul. *Everything You Need to Know About
  Mononucleosis* New York: The Rosen Publishing Group, 1998.

Web Sites

KidsHealth: What's Mono?
http://www.kidshealth.org/kid/talk/qa/mono.html

MedlinePlus Medical Encyclopedia: Mononucleosis
http://www.nlm.nih.gov/medlineplus/ency/article/000591.htm

U.S. Department of Health and Human Services, National
   Institute of Allergy and Infectious Diseases—Understanding
   the Immune System: How it Works
http://www.niaid.nih.gov/publications/immune/the_immune_
   system.pdf

U.S Food and Drug Adminitstration: When Mono Takes You Out
   of the Action
http://www.fda.gov/fdac/features/1998/398_mono.html

INDEX

Page numbers for illustrations are in **boldface**

ABOUT THE AUTHOR

Gretchen Hoffmann has always been fascinated by science and enjoys learning and writing about science- and health-related subjects. Her work on topics such as heart disease, oncology (the study of cancer), infectious diseases, and inflammatory diseases has been published in Scholastic's *Science World, The New York Sun* and *The New York Resident.* She holds degrees in Biomedical Journalism and Biological Science and has conducted molecular biology and virology research at Cornell University in Ithaca, New York. Currently, Ms. Hoffmann is a senior medical writer and editor at a medical education company in New York.